I0476864

Table of Contents

HOW TO MAKE A LIVING AS A
WRITER

K.M GRAMLICH

How To Make A Living As A Writer

K.M Gramlich

Introduction

Is being a writer your dream job? Probably not, but if it is, then the contents of this book are meant for you. This book is a viable guide for writers and is written with the aim of helping both freelancers and authors effectively build their career in writing. Who's a writer? It's important to be clear about the category of people referred to as writers. A writer is any individual with a creative mind for generating unique ideas, developing them and putting them down on paper in a systematic manner. If that is you, then you are reading the right book!

This guide is comprised of insights borrowed from existing facts and shared personal experiences of successful writers both of which are dedicated to those beginning the journey of writing. Many new writers are harboring a host of questions, worries and fears while venturing in the dark trying to make a living from writing, a talent that they possess, but they don't have anyone to guide and mentor them . When I started writing as a freelancer, I had never written an article before and I didn't have someone to guide me through the process. I had to learn everything alone and I felt that I was literally walking in the dark. I've made serious mistakes but with lots of determination I'm still building my career in writing with hopes of reaching great heights.

In this book various topics, ranging from how-to, tips, guides, and dos and don'ts, have detailed explanations that will give you courage to venture into writing with hope and optimism. Writing depends on your creativity and your skills. However, there are many other hidden factors that determine success in a writing career. That's why this book has been developed and made available to you, so you don't have to go through the same dark path alone. Let's walk through this journey together, and after reading this book, you'll know how to build your writing career. Ready to be a great writer? Read on!

CHAPTER ONE
Top Secrets of Writing Success

Whether you're planning to start writing as a freelancer or as a novelist it's important to understand a few of my **top secrets of writing success**. Through book or article writing you can make more money by uploading your books online or launching them on the selling platforms such as Amazon Kindle, Barnes and Nobel or eBay compared to traditional publishing. In addition there are websites such a Odesk, Fiverr and Elance where you can create an online profile and be hired for freelance work. Good writing improves your online profile, gaining you more contracts for writing books, journals and articles for other clients. This also becomes an added source of income. Let's now look at the top secrets for success in writing.

- *Identify your own voice*

In order to succeed in writing, it's vital to identify your own voice. This refers to the style that you portray your main ideas within your texts. Remember, that these ideas should be connected and provide a good flow for the reader. It's important to put aside certain writing rules as these can block the flow of thoughts. Examples of rules are, run on sentences or ending sentences in prepositions. When you put aside the rules in writing, you're more likely to have fun writing and not get tired, as some books feature many chapters that need to be covered. In this case, write the ideas as they come in either on a notebook or type them directly into a word document. Refraining from being tied down by writing rules enhances the passion for writing, and you just need to let your thoughts and creativity flow from your head into the book or article.

- *Value what you create*

Valuing what you create is a secret that most successful writers have discovered and implemented. Writing is one of the creative arts hence everything that you write down on paper is born out of creativity. The contents of the document you're writing should come right from your heart and should be an indication that you've given it the best creative power possible. Writing ideas from the heart differ from following someone else's creativity or ideas. When you decide to base your writing on another person's idea, there's a higher likelihood you'll abandon the whole project when fatigue and other challenges set in. Therefore, don't write articles or books because others are doing it. You may not value what you put into it. If you don't love a piece of work that you've written, then nobody will want to read it. Make sure to value your work!

- *Think positively*

Do you know why people with great ideas fail? It's because of negative thinking. If you don't motivate yourself, your reader won't either. As a writer, you need to develop positive thinking for yourself and translate this in your writing. Practicing positive thinking helps you focus more on the lighter side of each project than the possible failures you may occur. As a writer, I've learned how to think positively, even after a project that didn't go well or even if I'm having a lousy day. In this case, I always take it as a learning experience that strengthens and makes me a better writer for a future projects. Note that writing is more like a journey of discovery that can be halted by demoralizing thoughts. Don't criticize yourself. Criticisms are not good companions in this odyssey of being a writer.

● *Take what you can chew*

This is an old saying that you should relate to as a writer. This simply means engage in assignments that you can effectively handle. The last thing you want is negativity for your writing career if you overwhelm yourself. It's a good idea to take one assignment at a time and focus on being efficient and producing high quality work. I interviewed John a freelance writer who mentored me in my writing career. He's a prolific writer and an author on several freelancing sites; I discovered that recently he took a one year break from writing. He made this decision due to the fact he started to suffer from burnout. He was accepting huge assignments within a very limited time.

John says this, "I thought getting more contracts and large assignments would lead to more earnings. I just didn't have the time to keep up. I ended up not meeting set deadlines for two of the assignments while one of the assignments I had delivered earlier was rejected due to poor quality. I was demoralized when I realized I had lost three assignments in the process. The feeling of loss and fatigue put me down and I lost interest in writing for several months. It was a difficult process getting back to my earlier position. Today, I decline some requests or negotiate for a more flexible and achievable deadline. This has improved my profile, quality of my work and lifestyle."

● *Do not stop…..keep writing*

It doesn't matter how slow you move so long as you don't stop! This is such a rich saying that should be your mantra in making your writing dreams come true. This helps you fight procrastination. Don't say that you're tired; sit down and write a paragraph. It will increase the amount of work completed. I have learned this in my writing journey as sometimes I just want to take a day off and relax due to perceived low energy. I always value the few lines that I write on days like this instead of struggling to write pages. This forms a new starting point the next day when I'm full of energy to complete several pages. You may be discouraged if you're a slow typest in the beginning. When I started, I was writing approximately 500 words in three hours but as I took more projects and started practicing more, I gained speed. Today I can type up to 1000 words in one hour.

The most important thing is to evaluate your current typing speed and energy then set realistic targets. Whichever the case, keep moving, do not stop!

● *Do not compare your achievement with the achievements of others*

Do you want to kill your dream of being a successful writer? Well, keep comparing your achievement with those from others. This is a poisonous sting that lames your writing career, especially if you compare your progress with novelists who've been in the field for decades. This doesn't make you a legend rather it discourages you. Instead of comparing yourself to others, identify a writer of a few best selling books whose writing style appeals to you and let them mentor you. This can be done directly through one on one communication or indirectly by reading some of their works and learning from them. Remember that writing is an amazing artistic journey where progress is measured based on the individual.

In order to utilize the above secrets for a successful writing career, it is important to consider the main tips for top selling articles and books as discussed in the next chapter.

CHAPTER TWO
Essential Elements in a Writing Career

Are you looking forward to building a successful career? There are essential elements that you'll need to consider within the writing process. In a writing career, the most important person is you, as you are the one spearheading the writing process and putting in place the infrastructure to ensure that the published work finds its way to the market. The elements to consider depend on what type of writing you are doing. If you're an author, it's important to identify partners to help you navigate the publishing market. On the other hand, as a freelancer engaged in article writing, you'll need to have a blog or identify a platform where your services can be hired by people running online businesses. Essential elements in writing career include:

1. Developing a line of thought

The line of thought developed gives an individual writer a unique identity. The line of thought developed can be traced throughout the person's work. This element helps you as a writer to identify a niche you can thrive in. If you're planning to succeed as an author it's important to know whether your line of thought leads to writing a fiction or non-fiction book or generating books based on a particular career or motivational materials. On the other hand, as a freelancer, it's important to develop your line of thought and identify whether you are good at writing information based articles, procedure guides or materials with some sort of sales tone. This helps channeling your energy and guides you to find that specific niche you're more likely to thrive in.

2. Identifying the target audience

When writing it's important to identify your target audience. This entails determining the population that's likely to benefit from your message. Knowing your audience helps with setting the tone within the article or book and can easily convey the information. The audience can be within a given age bracket, different genders, within a variety of career groups, or people just looking for a specific need or service. Once you accurately identify the target audience, it's much easier to write materials that are relevant to them.

3. Plan the outline of the book or article

In order to effectively write in a way that gives your reader reason to continue through your work, it's essential to make a good plan and have some sort of outline of the entire document. In this case, you need to come up with an eye catching title that attracts the reader and peruses them to continue through your article or book. A brief introduction that highlights details covered in the work, an easy to ready body that connects well with the title, and a conclusion that wraps up the entire work. If you're writing a book, the body should be in chapter form while an article covers different segments. A well done outline and detailed plan helps in ensuring a good flow throughout the book or articles. This makes the readers want to continue.

4. Market your work

Marketing is a vital area and is essential in making your work known in the market. If you've written a book, marketing entails carrying out a market research in order to track the current trends in the book selling platforms. This should be followed by launching the book online through your own site or a hosting website. When dealing with article writing, owning or forming a partnership with a blog site is essential in making yourself known as a prolific writer. In addition, it's important to build your profile if you are a member of a working platform.

I interviewed June working on oDesk. June started from scratch and now has over 100 positive reviews from clients and she had this to say,

"Hi, my name is June. My journey as a freelancer has not been easy especially in the beginning but today I am reaping the fruits of my hard work. When I started, I did not have a single review on my profile. I started imagining possible article topics and writing them in order to have something to show for the clients to hire me. When I got my first client three weeks after signing in an account, I decided to commit myself to delivering quality work and observing the deadlines. This has made me grow as a writer with a very attractive profile that tells the prospect clients what I can offer for their projects to be successful. I have learned to be patient making little steps each time while learning from every experience. I wish to encourage other writers to keep believing that you can. Determination and commitment lead to great success as today I am hired even without having applied for a job."

Building an attractive profile that reflects skills, potentials, professionalism and experience is a powerful marketing tool for the writers.

CHAPTER THREE
How to Reach Your Goals as a Writer

Goals refer to what you want to achieve within a given period of time in a writing career. Goals should not be hard to achieve as long as the due process is used. The starting point of achieving the goals is having a positive attitude towards the project. This entails having positive thoughts that sends positive vibes into your work that no set goals are impossible to achieve. As you put effort in making a project successful, here are some of the steps in achieving goals set for   a writing career.

- ***Be specific***

Stating your goals in a specific manner helps in achieving them easily. In order to translate the dream of becoming a successful writer into a tangible goal that can be implemented in terms of a plan, it's important to state the goals in operational or 'doing' words. This entails breaking the goals into small steps that can be accomplished each at a time. This is essential in allowing a direct management of the set goals. In this case, you should use words that generate tasks that have to be performed. In addition, be specific and clear about what you want to achieve.

For example when I started my journey into the writing career, I set two goals one of them was to develop my writing skills through practice and the other was to complete two projects on writing web content for new sites within a month. In this case, I was clear on what I wanted to achieve and this guided me in the type of jobs I was applying for. In three weeks I had achieved the goals. I provided web contents for three new websites each having a minimum of five web pages. I also improved greatly in learning how to fix multiple keywords in an article for site optimization while previously I was only conversant in fixing a single keyword. This was a great achievement and it gave me confidence in handling projects that I had no experience in.

- ***Make measurable goals***

In order to succeed in achieving goals it's important to measure. Having goals that are measurable is vital as it aids in accountability of your efficiency in this career. This can be in terms of defining the amount of money you wish to make within a given period of time and where you want to be after a period of writing. I interviewed Eva a freelance writer with regards to setting measurable goals and she had the following to say;

> *"Setting of measurable goals has led to great success in my career writing. I normally set short term goals as I am growing in skills and experience each day. I do this by setting targets in terms of money I want to make within a week. For example if my target is to make $150 within a week, I ensure that I work hard towards that because it is a measurable goal. In addition, I do set limited time within which I have to complete the assignments regardless of the long deadlines set by the clients. In this case, if I have 5 articles with 500 words each, I ensure that it is done within a maximum of 7 hours. This helps in leaving adequate time free to*

handle any other assignment that may come by. These two measurable goals are related as the quick turnarounds make it possible for me to make the target amount of money. Setting goals that are measurable has enabled me to meet my targets and grow career wise."

● *Set a time-line for goals*

Goals that are time bound are easy to achieve. This basically means setting a time-line to the set goals so that they are to be achieved within a specific period of time. Goals without any specific time attached to them may not be achieved as they are subject to postponement. Setting a time-frame on the specific goals enhances efficiency while putting procrastination at bay. Once the set time-frame is half way gone, an evaluation should be done to determine the goals that have been achieved so far as well as the ones yet to be achieved and what is needed to achieve them. Setting personal deadlines that are different from those of the client you are working for helps in remaining focused on an overall purpose.

● *Be realistic*

When setting goals as a writer it is important to be realistic. This leads to setting goals that are achievable within your means. Depending on the level of your skills and experience you can evaluate how much you can achieve within a specific given period of time. This helps you not to set goals that are too high or too low for your competence. I did this one time when I set goals that were too ambitious in my writing career. I set a goal of typing 5000 words within six hours and at this time I was still struggling to gain considerable typing speed. This led into picking more jobs than I could handle within a day. Though I struggled through the 3 assignments, I had to work over 24hours to complete them. This goal was not realistic as I did not consider my skills and experience before setting it. Today, I always evaluate the resources I have in terms of time at hand and skills to make realistic goals. Also, do not forget the countries with electric power issues which is common in African and Asian countries among others. Therefore, you need to check whether you reside in any of the countries with such a problem as it is likely to interfere with your work. In addition, you should consider the internet connectivity as it is vital in achieving the set goals. This leads to setting goals that are achievable without straining or overrating yourself.

● *Create an accountability system*

In order to achieve the goals set for the growth of a writing career, it is important to create an accountability system. This applies whether you are a freelance article or a book author. Remember that this is a private business in which you are the manager, supervisor and task person on the ground. In this case, it is advisable to let someone else know what you want to achieve in a writing career. However, you need to be careful not to confide in people who are likely to put you down, rather the individual should be business oriented with great leadership characteristics. This is an individual who will encourage you in the process of establishing your writing career and correct you when you follow the wrong path. When you let someone else know what you are aiming at, you are likely to be committed to the set goals.

• *Design a strategic plan*

Designing a strategic plan derived from the set goals is important in achieving them. Remember that setting goals and doing nothing about them means that they just remain on the paper. Once through with goal setting it is important to draw a strategic plan that entails a plan of action that leads to reaching the goal. This plan provides a clear way on how to go about achieving the goals. The plan comprises of the implementation process based on the specific project to be accomplished in line with the goals, the time required and the resources involved. This leads to successful achievement of the goals.

CHAPTER FOUR
How to Increase Writing Speed

Besides creativity, writing speed is a key skill required for a successful career. Many people believe that writing speed only covers the actual typing. Well, this is partially true as the speed of writing is determined by the preparation made prior to the actual writing. Increasing the speed of writing is important in book, article and report writing. This can also graduate you to being a news writer as they are aired within a strict time frame. You need to note that failure to meet the agreed upon deadlines in article writing may lead to destruction of your profile. In addition, lack of adequate speed may result in failure to launch a book as planned. Here are some tips that will help you increase your writing speed.

● *Do research in advance*

In any form of writing whether news, articles or a book, research for the relevant information to be included in the script is essential. This process has been made easier by the availability of adequate materials online. It is advisable to research the main topic by exploring the different titles to be included in the book. In this case, you need to break the main topic into subtitles making it easy to carry out the research and later write the book based on those subtitles. When writing an article, you need to research the topic getting different perspectives of the topic. When I am writing articles requested by clients I prefer researching the night before I start the writing process. If I am to write 10 articles, I make sure that before I sleep I have all the related information that I need for successfully writing the articles. This helps me to become familiarized with the topics involved, sleep on them and just put them down once I wake up the following day. This has always helped me to write fast.

● *Structure the work into small chunks*

This entails defining the structure of a particular chapter in the book or an article. This is made successful by writing down the key points to be discussed in a given chapter or in the article. In this case, it is advisable to identify the points to write first for a good flow. Writing the points down also helps you in organizing your thoughts before starting to type the work. Now, once you start the actual writing your thoughts will just flow. If writing a book, you should handle each chapter one at a time to avoid an overlapping of ideas that are likely to slow your writing speed.

● *Get rid of distractions*

The greatest enemies at this stage of writing are the distractions. Once you are distracted, you are likely to lag behind the set schedule and lose a very important unwritten thought you wanted to include in the article or the chapter of the book. In addition, it takes time for you to get back on track of writing after being distracted thus slowing your writing speed. The first step in curbing this is to identify the distractions and eliminating them. I interviewed Carol who is a freelance news writer for a television network and she had this to say about distractions;

"In the first two months of my career in news writing I risked losing my job for almost missed deadlines and inconsistencies. I made a decision to get rid of all the distractions that were blocking my writing process. I had to manage my email, phone, Skype, my interesting TV shows and other live chats as they are major sources of distraction. I have succeeded in effectively eliminating these distracters by waking up early in the morning to check mails and respond to any urgent messages. I also ensure that I send text messages to the people I need to communicate with during the day indicating the time that I will be available to discuss matters of concern with them. After this, I operate as if the communication devices do not exist. In addition, I avoid watching programs that are aired in series that connect to each other as they can easily hook me hence getting addicted. This has helped me to manage distractions effectively and write faster."

• *Set mini time-line*

A mini time-line refers to the amount of work you need to do within a specific time frame before taking a break. Before starting to write in the beginning of the day you need to have a working timetable that will help in striking a balance between your writing career and other chores. This is essential for work at home moms with little kids to take care of. Define when you need to drop and pick up kids in/from school, breastfeed your baby and fix meals for the family. This mini time-line worked so well for me especially in the second year of my writing career when I delivered my first born. I had to set time aside to attend and breast feed him. During this period I discovered the importance of setting a mini time-line that corresponded with the feeding time of my baby. I never missed any deadlines for the assignments entrusted to me for I knew when to write continuously and when to take a break and be with my little son. You can create a mini time-line that suits your program and ensure that you are realistic enough. This helps in enhancing your writing speed.

• *Breaks are important*

Take breaks, they are important for active thinking. Most people take a break when they are tired and too exhausted to continue. This should not be the case, as it takes a lot of time for one to recover and get back to work. The best way to go about it is to take a break before you get tired! In this case, you need to evaluate your concentration span and the period of time you can sit continuously and comfortably work. The break should come as soon as you feel the need to stand in order to have a stretch and when your concentration starts to go down. Do not force yourself to work at this point but take a break. I normally take a break of thirty minutes after every three hours of working with an afternoon nap in which I do not have to sleep but just relax for around one hour. This is essential in getting refreshed and working with the same speed that you began with in the morning. This leads to quality work at the end of the day and fast writing.

• *Learn to walk away*

In order to succeed as a writer, you need to learn when and how to walk away! Getting blocked or stuck in the writing process is a normal experience for every writer. You will not complete a book or numerous articles without getting stuck or feeling blocked. When this happens to you do not panic or force yourself to write out the contents, simply walk away. In this case, you can take a walk in your favorite park to enjoy nature or take up a short activity among your hobbies. If this happens towards evening, close your work for that day and sleep on the idea you were trying to develop when you got stuck or blocked. When you walk away and then start working again, ideas will start flowing once again as it helps your brain to get refreshed once more hence writing faster.

CHAPTER FIVE
Tips on Unlocking Your Creativity

Creativity is an essential requirement in a writing career as it is an art. Creativity refers to your ability to create a new and unique piece of work while effectively solving the problem and adapting to the change. Creativity goes beyond creating new things to seeing possibilities in challenging situations that you will face in your career as a writer. Many people shy away from embracing a writing career because they think that they are not creative enough. These thoughts might be bogging your mind and limiting you from going ahead and venturing into this noble career. Well, the truth is that you are creative but disconnected from your creative mind. This disconnection can also happen during the writing process hence getting stuck or stagnant. Good news is that you can unlock your creativity thus getting reconnected once again. Let us explore effective ways of unlocking your creativity.

1. Create a habit of discomfort

In order to be highly creative you need to move away from your comfort zone. It is sweet to be in your comfort zone but it locks your creativity. At this point, it becomes impossible for you to unleash your full potential as a writer. This is why you need to create a habit of getting really uncomfortable once the career seems to be highly productive for this is the best time to proceed to the next level. This simply means that when all the current challenges have been overcome and the project has been accomplished in form of a published book that is doing well in the market, it is time to celebrate yes, but also the prime moment to draft a new project. It is advisable to think of a new project once the current book is launched so that at the same time you will be getting into celebratory mode you will be launching the new project as well. This unlocks your creativity before actually getting stuck.

2. Change the environment

Change of the environment is one of the effective ways of unlocking creativity. This entails temporary moving from your current location to another. This can be for some hours, some days or a few weeks. To start, you need to identify that place with scenery that helps you relax and inspires you. The duration depends on how intense the situation is. In this case, it can vary from a simple walk to a full holiday. If you are writing a complex novel, it is important at some point to hibernate in a different environment in order to complete it as you are likely to get stuck, dry or blocked at some point. It is necessary to unlock your creativity once you have completed one project and ready for another by taking a vacation over a weekend or for few weeks. This helps you in getting inspired hence unlocking creativity.

3. Perform imagery exercise

In order to unlock your creativity, you need to allow yourself to perform imagery exercises. Remember that creativity is an intensive mental process that requires to be revitalized after a period of time. Imagery exercises entail daydreaming which most people might consider time wasting. However, each imagery exercise should be structured to fall on a specific and appropriate time. It is advisable to be in a quiet environment then close your eyes and let your mind go wild. If you are distracted by other serious thoughts that are not related to creativity, imagine putting them in a basket and dashing them into the air to vanish. This helps you to enjoy a host of ideas that flows through your mind and you may be amazed coming up with a new writing project from a single daydreaming session. If you allow yourself to daydream without getting distracted, you gain the most enjoyable experience that unlocks your creativity.

4. Take risks

Creativity is all about risking putting your wild ideas out there to be read by a multitude of people. This requires great courage as you do not know how other people will interpret your ideas and what their comments might be. Taking risks is essential for both the book authors and article writer. Remember that in the industry you will have haters and lovers hence knowing how to handle them effectively is important in risking and unlocking your creativity. In order to know if a risk is worth taking, it is advisable to share your idea with your mentor who may suggest some changes to improve it. Then, evaluate the impact of that idea if it is welcome by the readers. In the same way, determine the worst thing that can happen if the readers criticize it. At the same time, during the thinking process to generate the required ideas, avoid labeling of the creative thoughts that comes up as silly or nonsensical as this is likely to block your creativity. Therefore, shut all the judgments and what if statements and let the ideas flow freely.

5. Let your inner child out

Children are highly creative until they start receiving negative feedback that shuts their creative minds down. Well, we all have our inner child within us regardless of our chronological age or experiences in life. Letting your inner child out is the best way of unlocking creativity. You can achieve this by taking time to play and have fun while locking your serious self in a different compartment. This becomes effective if you have small kids in the house as you can take at least one hour daily to play and laugh with them by participating in their games. In addition, you can connect with your paddies to play games in an environment in where you can laugh freely and be childlike. You can also link up with a person you are close to watch a fun filled film or movie. This can be part of your unwinding process after a long day writing or at the end of the week. This helps in unlocking your creativity hence generating new and unique ideas that makes your work standout.

6 Affirm yourself

In order to succeed in your writing career, it is important to learn how to affirm yourself. This is essential because not all the time will you have people around to affirm you. Self affirmation comes in handy when your creativity is blocked, either after a complex writing project or locked by unhealthy criticism right, left and center. Remember that you become who you think and believe you are. Therefore, make self affirmation your daily habit. This helps you to nurture thoughts that enhance your creative ability. Develop mantras that are geared towards promoting your creativity such as "I am creative. Creativity is my way of life. My creative ideas are varied," among others. You can come up with short sentences and stick the m on the wall of your bedroom and on the stirring wheel of the car. This plays a great role in affirming yourself as the mantras become part of you hence unlocking your creativity.

7. Stay away from digital devices

When pursuing you writing career, you cannot stay away from digital devices for you need them for your work. However, these devices can be a block to unlocking your creativity as they are a major source of distraction from paying attention to your thought system. Therefore, it is advisable to designate time when you switch off all the digital devices in your house starting with the mobile phone, computer, television, music system and any other devices around. Once this is done, just have a nature walk, gaze out through the window or just sit in the house listening, watching or doing nothing. This helps you to listen to your inner self and inspiration that comes from it thus unlocking your creativity. Jaclyn is a successful writer in one of the freelancing platforms and she has this to say about the impact of staying away from digital devices:

"I have written eBooks for many clients based on different topics. Sometimes I get stuck and blocked in the writing process that might be disturbing because of the tight deadlines set by the clients. I shared this challenge with a friend of mine where I revealed that I like working in a room filled with soft music. He encouraged me to switch off all the digital devices in the house when I feel blocked and I cannot write any more and gaze outside through the window or I close my eyes and relax in silence. This has since then worked for I take about one hour in total silence. This helps me to refocus with refreshed creativity that brings about new ideas for the book."

Identifying the above tips that work best in unlocking your creativity is important as each person is different. Unlocking your creativity results in a great writing career.

CHAPTER SIX
How to Nurture and Maintain Resilience

Resilience is the spirit of being relentless in facing tough moments. This is basically the ability to bounce back without harboring feelings of self pity or helplessness that make you a victim of the situation. Helplessness or seeing yourself as a victim of circumstances works against your writing career dream as it blocks the creativity and drains the energy that would have been used to overcome the current challenges. Nurturing and maintain resilience is essential in a writing career as it helps you in raising above the stress that can be overwhelming while reducing chances of getting into a depression that is a threat to the thriving of a writing career. As a writer, resilience makes it possible to embark on another project after a previous one has been termed as a total failure and locked by stinging criticism. Maintaining resilience helps you to move on with purpose, renewed energy to make things right and live happily despite failed projects. I believe you want to nurture your resilience, so let us explore the following tips together;

- *Develop a positive attitude*

Later in this book, we will discuss more ways of developing positive attitudes. However, positive attitudes are essential in nurturing resilience especially in those tough times in your writing career. A writing project can fail when the client does not approve of your work for article writing, in which you have spent hours and a lot of energy accomplishing or the book in which you have invested a lot of resources is rejected in the market by readers. In either case, as a writer you are likely to get demoralized by the situation and wanting to quit the career. Though there might be criticism attached to the failure, some of which might be on social media platforms hence accessible by a multitude globally, you can raise again through a positive attitude. This entails a conscious process as shared by Augustine J. in his journey as a freelance writer;

> *"My initial steps in freelancing career were bumpy and turbulent. I almost quit writing to start a different business as my first three projects were rejected by clients on quality basis. My profile had very poor rating and reviews. When the third project was rejected I got stressed up and felt that I did not have energy even to type half a page of another project that I was handling. I booked myself for one hour counseling session with a professional counselor who guided on how to nurture resilience within me. I started sensing negative thoughts way before I could process them and I would come up with about two different positive thoughts to counteract the upcoming negative one. In addition, instead of spending time alone, I identified friends with positive attitudes towards life and I started hanging out with them. I kept off writing for one then I bounced back with a purpose and renewed energy to move on. Today, I have 72 positive reviews with a 4.95 rating on my profile. This does not mean that I do not fail sometime, but I am resilient in my career hence overcoming all the challenges."*

Therefore, consciously nurture and maintain resilience to succeed in writing.

- ***Be open minded***

It is human nature to resist change instead of embracing a new situation. This blocks one from exploring the opportunities that comes with the newness. You can only embrace change if you are open minded enough to step out of your comfort zone. It is important to note that writing is full of uncertainties that require continuous adjustments in order to remain relevant to the target audience. If you are a freelance writer, then change will truly be a constant in your entire career as each client has their own expectations for your work. Personally, I was very rigid and always wanted to do things in the same way I was comfortable with. Well, this had to change when I embarked on writing as I had to interpret exactly what my clients need done in their projects and owning those projects in order to deliver the complete assignment as desired. Well, this does not always work as projects are still rejected. When this happens, I have leaned not to blame myself or any other person for the failed project and avoided creating a big mountain out of a mole hole as it was not the end of the world. This helps me to remain open minded hence embracing changes proposed by the clients and other mentors around me. This helps me not to spend my energy on the failed project, rather to learn from the mistakes and being open minded to focus my energy on other projects.

- ***Search for the light side***

In order to nurture and maintain resilience in a writing career, it is vital to search for the light side in any given situation. You should make it a habit not to concentrate on the problem rather than the solutions to it. Focusing so much on the challenges drains the energies you would have used to enact solutions to the problem at hand while blocking you from seeing the opportunities that are beyond the problem. To succeed in a writing career, you need to develop a habit of discovering the positive side of a challenge or a major problem. This helps you in bouncing back after a tough time even if you had to take a break from writing for a while to revitalize yourself. Searching for the light side in a dark period may open up a new horizon that makes your dream in writing career come true.

- ***Increase your knowledge***

Increasing your knowledge gives you an edge in handling the challenges associated with writing. Today it is easy to increase your knowledge as eBooks, journals and articles on varying topics are available online. It is a good idea to make reading of these materials from internet to be part of your leisure activities as it can enhance the nurturing of resilience. In addition, some recorded talks of motivational speakers are posted on YouTube and you can plan to listen to a portion of the conference either before sleeping or early in the morning for inspiration. This helps in strengthening your problem solving ability and providing added strategies of surviving in the difficult times of your writing career. When seeking to increase your knowledge you can read about the lives of authors of bestselling books thus borrowing a leaf from their journey in writing careers, especially how they triumphed during the turbulent seasons. This helps in nurturing and maintaining resilience.

● *Take good care of yourself*

When running a business with several employees, your productivity depends on how well you treat the human resource. The same happens in a writing career, remember that you are the major human resource in this job. Therefore, provide good care to yourself by paying attention to all the faculties of your being. In this case, you need to take care of your physical body through regular exercise, observing a proper diet and taking enough rest. It is advisable to allocate a free day in a week to unwind by deciding not even to open the computer and stay away from writing. In addition, you need to take care of your emotional life by surrounding yourself with people who truly love and appreciate you. Everyone has their own spirituality including you. Therefore, take time to meditate in silence in order to feed your inner self. This helps in nurturing and maintaining resilience that leads to success in your writing career. When interviewing Eva K. a freelance writer concerning taking good care of self and she had this to share;

> *"I suffered a major burnout in year 2013 because of working without taking time to rest. I had a lot of writing assignments such that I completely forgot myself. I had two weeks of intensive work in which finding time to eat was hectic. I visited my doctor at the end of the two weeks as I felt sickly and weak. The doctor advised me to take complete bed rest for one day and later he advised me on observing a healthy lifestyle that entails daily physical exercises, healthy diet and good rest at night. As a freelancer, I always let my clients know that I do not work on Sundays as this is my free day. This has helped me to have the ability to face daily challenges in my career as a writer."*

● *Work on your self-esteem*

Your self-esteem is the bedrock of courage and assertiveness. Remember that as an author of books, you will have to face some haters who will criticize your entire work, sometimes for no credible reason at all. The more popular you become the worse the criticism is likely to get, such that you may wake up in the morning and find that negative news about you has been trending in the social media platform for the past few hours. On the other hand as a freelance writer, you will meet some clients who are bullies with a bad attitude towards you. In any of the cases, if your self-esteem is low, the comments and bullying attitude will definitely make you sink into the deepest hole of self. This is a real threat to your career so you need to work on self-esteem.

In this case, you can just let the trending news about you continue without reacting to it but take note of the areas that you need to improve and work on. The trending comments about you are likely to bring more followers into your site if you have one or more social media accounts. Instead of whining, focus on that positive side of the trending malicious comments concerning your work. If you are a freelancer working with a bullying client, it is important to have healthy self-esteem that helps you to be assertive in communicating with the client on what you need and sometimes to opt out of a project if there is no respect. Good and healthy self-esteem leads to well grounded and maintained resilience that gives you the ability to overcome all the challenges in your writing career.

CHAPTER SEVEN
Ways of maintaining a Positive Attitude

Positive attitude is the ability to accept the current situation without whining or self pity. This gives deep peace to your inner self, deep fulfillment and the ability to remain positive in difficult moments. Being a successful writer does not mean that you will be happy or satisfied if you do not have positive attitude. In addition, failure to maintain a positive attitude especially in the beginning of the writing career, makes it difficult to go through the humble beginnings as you are likely to get discouraged. Therefore, having a positive attitude in writing and life in general is important as it leads to great success. Here are effective tips that will help you in maintaining a positive attitude towards life and a career as a writer.

1. Let your day start early

Starting the day early is very important in enhancing your positive attitude. Starting your day early in the morning, helps in achieving extra things in life without interfering with your planned writing assignments. It is advisable to start the day by having body exercises and then settling down to listen to the motivational materials. There are podcasts and DVDs with very rich recorded motivational talks that you can take few minutes in the morning to listen to. Many people argue that it is not easy to rise early and prefer taking more time bargaining in bed. If you are not accustomed in rising early it is possible to gradually make it a habit. For example, you can start by waking up one hour earlier and continue programming your morning like that till when you are used to the system. Ida had a struggle waking up in the morning before 8am and this is what she has to share with us;

> *"I am a freelance writer handling assignments related to article writing for magazines, news and web content. When I started on this career, I could not rise up before 8am as I had stayed at home without a job for almost one year. I missed several contracts because of waking up rate while not having enough time to do anything meaningful. I shared this struggle with Kate a friend of mine and an experienced writer who advised me to try waking up half an hour earlier but I still bargained too much and being late all the same. She then advised to me to wake one hour earlier which was very successful because at least I had few minutes to roll on the bed and wake up earlier than 8am. I put a lot of effort and today I do not have to set the alarm but I automatically rise up at 3.30am every morning, to exercise for 45 minutes, freshen up with 15 minutes then I listen to a motivational speech for about 10 minutes before now sitting down to start my day. Now I have a young family and I do not rush against time to have the chores done in order to meet the deadlines in my writing career."*

You can develop and maintain a positive attitude in your writing career and life in general, if you assume a habit of starting your day early.

2. Have a weekly plan of activities

Failure to plan is an effective plan to fail while harboring negative attitudes in life as you are likely to be busy responding to eventualities. This is uncalled for as planning for the activities of the week helps you in foreseeing different events that you need to attend to and the time available for the eventualities if any. In this case, it is advisable to have each day in the week planned for including that free day. Well, it is one thing to plan and another to adhere to the laid down plan. Thus, in order for the weekly plan to be effective it is important to stick to the schedule unless an unforeseen emergency arises, which is normally once in a while. This helps in proper time management so that you do not get under pressure to complete daily tasks. Remember that pressure arising from incomplete tasks leads to anxiety and tension that matures to stress hence the negative attitude in all that you do. Therefore, work smart by planning your week for relaxed moments that results in building up of a positive attitude towards your writing career and life. In addition, this leads to achieving the weekly goals that bring about fulfillment and happiness in your career.

3. Be positive, expect the unexpected

Change is the only constant in life. It is important to know that not everything will work as planned or as you wish each day. The expectation to succeed and achieve the goals each day throughout the year is unrealistic. Therefore, expect flops in the process and prepare yourself to handle them as they come for you cannot tell when they will show up. You can successfully handle the unforeseen changes by being positive and flexible to adapt to any change. This can be a change in the planned activities of the day caused by other eventualities without becoming anxious or angry as this will drain your energy, causing you to have a negative attitude for the day.

> In most parts of Africa there are issues with electricity especially during the rainy seasons. You would agree with me without electric power, I am rendered jobless as a freelance writer. In the beginning, I would not plan for the power blackouts but they did happen anyway and I would get really mad about it. This was giving me bad days and being negative about achieving my goals in writing. Today, I always expect that there is a likely hood of experiencing power blackout within the week that might even take a whole day. In this case, instead of waiting for the blackouts and getting angry about it, I ensure that I am efficient in completing my assignments including those with an extended deadline way before the due time such that if there is no power my work is not negatively affected. In addition, when there is a power blackout, I always adjust my plan for the day and carryout other tasks that I would have handled later in the day or scheduled for another day such as housekeeping chores or shopping. This helps in saving time hence achieving my goals. Being flexible and positively embracing change helps me to maintain positive attitude in my writing career and life.

Be positive, expect the unexpected for happiness and fulfillment in your career due to an enhanced positive attitude!

4. Form a positive social network

As the saying goes, no man is an island, forming a positive social network is vital not only for your life but for your career. Remember that the nature of your social network can either enhance positive attitude in you or influence you negatively. The catch here is getting connected with people who are positive about life and their career no matter what. These are people who have gone through trying moments in life and emerged victorious, they are likely to motivate you to soldier on in your writing career. We all unconsciously spread positive or negative vibes to those around us. Well, expect the same from your social network as they can either promote positive or negative attitudes depending with their personal perceptions in life. Therefore, connect yourself with people who have a positive attitude in life for they are likely to motivate you during those bad days in your life and career. Humor is a good source of positive attitude. Thus, get people who have the ability to come up with humor in an ugly situation to lighten the moment and laugh about it. This is exactly the type of social network you need around you, it is worth it!

5. *Get spiritually connected*

Spirituality is part of our life as it connects us to our higher being. Being spiritually connected simply means strengthening the link you have with your higher being. It doesn't matter which your religion but within you there is the ability to identify your spirituality. Read few lines of the scripture or inspirational texts that speak to your spirit. Others get spiritually connected through soft music that you can play through your music system or the background of your computer, when you do not have complex work, this can help. Getting spiritually connected helps in enhancing a positive attitude towards life and your writing career as well.

CHAPTER EIGHT
How to Write Novels in 30 Days

Writing a novel is a process that when followed is easy to achieve the set target. Do you know why your novel is written in your head but not on the paper? It is lack of a decisive action to transfer the ideas from your head to the paper. Novel writing may seem to be the most difficult task to perform. Well, the truth is that having the ideas is the most difficult task and the fact that they are present in the brain means the task is half way complete. The next half is writing the ideas down on paper and adding something fresh into them when typing the entire work. If you take a decisive action to sit down and write the ideas down, you can complete a novel within 3-4 weeks! Here is how to go about it practically;

- *Gather the appropriate tools*

In order to succeed writing a novel within a month, it is important to gather all the appropriate tools required in the process. This includes acquiring a computer and good internet connection in case you need to do research. It is advisable to get a laptop as you can write your novel wherever you go but a desktop can also serve the purpose. A good internet connection is also essential for effective communications with the support system in the process of writing the novel. In addition, it is important to ensure that you get external storage devices for the complete sections of the novel. The greatest frustration can result from the lost data of the complete work due to technical issues with the computer or a mistake in commanding a task in the system. It is advisable to save your complete work even though it is not refined in the external storage devices for retrial when needed.

- *Talk about your idea*

You may be surprised to discover that lack of a decisive action to start writing the novel arises from unfounded fears within you. Talking to another person about your idea helps you to address the resistances that block you from writing the novel. It is very important to identifying the right person to convey your idea to. The person should be trustworthy as you are to reveal your ideas to him or her in order to explore the path to successful writing together. Beware of the people who are likely to discourage you or get your ideas and develop their own novels launching it before you roll out yours. This has happened to others and it can happen to you hence the need to be careful. Also, the individual should be good at taking risks. This is a person who can help you to move from the comfort zone into the world unknown. The person you talk to helps you to move your plan to the next level.

- *Draw the structure of the novel*

Writing a novel is among the categories of the creative arts. It is important to come up with a real structure of the novel. This is guided by the ideas that you want to incorporate in the novel. Therefore, writing all the ideas down on paper and planning how to put the ideas across is essential. To start with, you need to come up with the title of the novel. This might be challenging so it is important to research for a possible title online to get ideas. The idea here is not to copy from others as you need to be creative and unique. An online search provides a good platform to brainstorm for the title, and later coming up with an eye catching title. In this case, do not get a title that is obvious but the one that makes the readers want to read your work.

Once you have settled for the title, it is time to come up with the characters. The major idea of what you want to write about should automatically suggest the main characters. When you positively identify the main characters, the others can be added as you continue writing the novel. In order to effectively come up with adequate characters who will build the story in the novel, it is advisable to let your mind to freely run the whole story like a movie that you have watched and taking note of the possible characters. This is possible after unlocking your creativity ability as discussed earlier. In this case, set yourself free to daydream.

● *Define the word count target*

Before starting to write a novel, it is important to set the word count target. This defines clearly the total number of the words that will make up the novel. Setting the word count target is vital as it guides in determining the number of chapters to be included as well as how far the story should be developed. Defining the total word count also aids in setting the daily target in writing. In this case, you can set a realistic target of the words that you need to write per day in order to complete the novel in thirty days. This depends on your typing speed as you can target to write a minimum of 5000 words daily if you have considerable typing speed. In addition, the daily targets should be set in line with the due date when you should have a complete novel. Calculating the number of words to write each day makes it possible for you to write a novel in thirty days.

● *Set a trial period*

There is truth in the fact that practice makes perfect. Before writing a novel to launch in the public domain, it is advisable to write a mock novel within a month. This is important if you are new in the field of writing and are struggling in gaining the typing speed, putting ideas together and gaining the required confidence. Therefore, start writing at the beginning of the month without caring about the writing rules or the flow of the ideas in the book. However, put in the best you can in the process in order to make an accurate evaluation about your writing style and speed. Once the mock novel is complete, let your mentor read it and provide an honest review about the writing style, time covered and the general quality of the novel. Once this is complete, you are ready for the real novel that can be based on the mock novel. It is important to maintain the idea expressed in the mock novel as the feedback provided by the mentor will be instrumental for its success when launched after thirty days of writing.

● *Set treats for the achieved targets*

Setting attractive treats for the achieved targets makes you eager to hit the targets. This is a motivating factor for you to be committed to attaining the targets. For example, there are some television programs that I love watching especially. One comes on daily at 6pm while others are present during the weekends at night. I make these programs part of my treats for achieving the daily and weekly targets so that I will only watch them once I am through with the set target. If I have an assignment that I wanted to complete within the day or the week and I fail to achieve that target because of any given reason, then instead of watching I have to sit and complete the assignments. This motivates me to work hard towards achieving the set targets.

You can determine what you like most in terms of snacks, watching movies or listening to music and making them treats for achieving the targets. In addition, you can promise your close friends that you will throw a party once you finish the novel within thirty days. I guess you would not like to fail your friends so you will work hard in order to reach the target hence remaining true to them by throwing a party.

- *Take a break*

Once the novel is complete in thirty days, it is advisable to take a break. However, this break has some rules attached to it. The recommended break period should not be less than two weeks or more than one month. During the break period, you should not think about the novel you have written or talk about it to anyone. Even though you may engage in writing as a leisure activity, it is advisable to refrain from any assignment during this period. Once the break period is over, it is time to proofread the complete novel in order to edit it. This becomes easy as you look at the novel as a new book that you are not familiar with hence reading exactly what is written other than what you want written. This helps you to identify errors easily and correct them.

- *Get a second opinion*

When you have written a piece of work, it is possible to overlook some major errors especially those regarding the flow of the novel. This is why you need to identify a third party to read through your work. It is advisable to nominate a friend who is not a writer or not familiar with the topic you have written about in your novel. This is because the person should read and understand the book as a common individual not as a professional writer. This helps in receiving reliable feedback and suggestions to some changes that will make your novel easy to read for the target audience.

- *Give your mentor a chance to read the book*

This is the final stage of proofreading the complete novel. Your mentor being a professional writer should have a third eye that points out the areas that you need to work on to perfect the entire novel. Once your mentor has made recommendations, you need to work on them making the novel ready for publishing. This marks the end of the tedious journey of having completed the novel in thirty days. At this point, you need to appreciate your work and thank yourself for the achievements without criticizing yourself for the mistakes noted during the process. Instead, learn from those mistakes for better novel writing tomorrow.

CHAPTER NINE
Big Mistakes to Avoid in Writing Career

It is advisable to start your career as a writer by being a freelancer. This is because freelancing entails writing articles some as short as 200 words. This gives you a chance to gain writing skills while perfecting your creativity and graduating to an experienced author of volumes of books in the global market. However, in freelancing you are likely to face several challenges that are likely to expose you to making several serious mistakes. Remember that some of those mistakes may discourage you from taking your writing career to the next level. The fact that as a freelancer you are supposed to get projects from the clients, interpret what to achieve and owning that project in order to deliver the desired results. Some of the assignments require a lot of creativity as the client might not provide the topics you need to focus on but provides just a general idea that he or she want you to develop. Let us look at the top mistakes you need to watch out for in freelancing;

- *Accepting too many assignments*

Freelancing can be attractive due to the money that comes with it. When your profile is well built with many good reviews, you stand a high chance of being hired compared to beginners. This can be tempting as you get offers with good money attached to them while they appear like simple tasks to be handled within a short period of time. This may result in taking on more than you can handle. Purity, an experienced freelancer has the following to share concerning workload;

> *"I have discovered that the easiest way to kill my writing career is by accepting more assignments than I can handle. I was a victim to this temptation six months ago when I picked five huge assignments that were to be delivered within few days. I managed to finish four of the assignments while the fifth one I requested a friend to handle it. I got the money yes, but the experience was not interesting as I lost interest in writing for few weeks. I suffered a burnout while my family suffered since I did not have time to be with my 4 year old twin boys. I regret this moment because I could not go to drop and pick them from school for one week and I had to hire someone to do it on my behalf. Worse, I had to buy ready food for family dinner for some days and it was very expensive. At the end of the week when all was done and said, I was worn-out, distanced myself from my family and spent more on other services thus not gaining much from the projects as I expected."*

Apart from what Purity experienced, taking on too much work can lead to low quality work and missed deadlines that can destroy your profile. Therefore, accept only the workload that you can manage or negotiate for extended deadlines.

- *Disregarding deadlines*

Disregarding deadlines is one of the worst mistakes you can make in freelancing. Before a client checks the quality of your work, one will always wait to see if you can meet the set deadlines. Missing deadlines is a sign of being unprofessional, incompetent and a lack of respect to the client. This makes you lose credibility, which is a big deal! However, you might miss a deadline due to emergencies such as sickness or technical issues with your computer. In this case, do not wait till the eve of the due date to inform the client that something has gone wrong. Instead, write an email to the client and inform them of what is happening and that you might miss the deadline. If the client can still extend the deadline, fine but if the job is urgent then set the client free to give the assignment to another person.

Sometime back I had a client who extended the deadline with two weeks for an assignment that he had entrusted to me. It was an assignment of thirty articles and soon after finishing the first one, my computer crashed. The cost of having it repaired was almost that of buying a new one. I used my mobile phone to send an email to the client informing him that I would only get money to buy a new computer after one week. The client appreciated the fact that I communicated with him few hours after my computer had crashed. He extended the deadline within which I delivered the complete project.

However, this should not be a habit as clients don't like frequent excuses. Meet the deadlines for your writing career to grow!

• *Putting up with a bad client*

In freelancing the majority of the clients are very professional and kind. However, there are some clients who are just bad news. These are clients who will receive complete and good quality assignments and never pay for them on time. Well, there are times that clients may have issues with their banks hence not being able to pay in time and this is acceptable though it should not be a pattern. Also note that it is okay for the client to request for corrections but when this request is endless and diverting from the original project guidelines initially provided to you by the same client, it is unacceptable. In addition, it is important to watch out for a client giving a huge workload with unrealistic deadlines. The worst part of such a client is that they will not end the contract but continue to suffocate you with assignments that you can barely handle. When a client is exhibiting the above characteristics or being disrespectful, you need to get rid of them immediately. Though the project might be tempting because of the money, you might end up getting demoralized and losing interest in advancing your career in writing. Remember that you have a right to quit from such a contract with the client.

• *Accepting projects with low offers*

Freelancing is a professional service just like any other career. As a freelancer, you have a right to rates that are proportional to the workload and complexity of the particular assignment. Before you bid or accept a job offer, it is important to evaluate how much the project will cost you in terms of time spent, efforts made and internet used in the process. This helps you to know whether the project is worth the amount being offered or not. You need to be alert especially when working with a client on a fixed long term contract, as the first assignment might be proportional to the rates offered while the consecutive assignments might not be. The best way to go about this challenge is to negotiate with the client for a better pay and if this does not work, do not accept the project as it will be a big loss for you.

• *Market your freelancing services*

It is important to acquire marketing skills for the freelancing services that you offer to the clients. This can be through sending a simple thank you note to the client after every assignment. Normally, the client will pay for the project soon after receiving it. Once you have received the payment, it is essential to send a thank you email to the client expressing your wish to work with them on another project. In addition, it is a marketing strategy to communicate continuously with your client in order to keep them updated during the assignment. It is also advisable to communicate with former clients to find out if they have an upcoming project. This makes the clients you have worked with remember you in their future projects.

CHAPTER TEN
Tips on Effective Time Management for a Writer

Freelancing is an attractive career as it brings about deep fulfillment. This type of career does not involve routine as it entails accomplishing projects that might be similar but each of them being unique. In this case, as a freelancer you will be creating some new informative articles, web content or product description, among other things. In addition, this career exposes you to a lot of knowledge as you carry out research on different niches. However, freelancing demands more time as the projects are based on a set deadline and the amount you make each month depends on the number of projects completed. Considering that each day has 24 hours, it is important to learn how to manage time well as a freelancer. Time is a major resource in a writing career as no one will be there to monitor you, rather you will be your own boss. Time management draws a line between efficient freelancers and those who struggle to meet deadlines. Here are viable tips in effective time management for a writing career;

- *Plan for the projects at hand*

Planning for the projects at hand should be done every week. This entails calculating the number of articles required within the week while allocating time to each of the projects. In this case, you need to be aware of the deadlines set for each of the projects so that if some of the deadlines are tying then you should to plan to finish one of the assignments ASAP. This helps in knowing the days that are fully packed with the assignments and when you are likely to be free. This should be charted on a drawn timetable in order to have a basis to evaluate whether you should accept other projects within the week and the time available for them.

> *Planning for the projects at hand has worked for me in the writing career. This is because I always estimate the time required to finish a particular project by calculating the total word count and dividing it with 5a 00 word article. This helps me to allocate time to all the projects depending on their deadlines and assessing how many more projects I can accept or not within the week.*

However, adherence to the made plan is important for proper time management.

- *Define specific working hours*

Time management in a writing career is jeopardized by failure to define specific working hours. As a freelance writer or an author, it is important to set specific working hours in a day. Remember that the client is your boss but the only way he or she can supervise you is through the setting of deadlines. In this case, you become your own manager and supervisor. Therefore, you should set the time when you need to start working in the morning and when to stop. If the working hours, according to your timetable, begins at 7am that should be observed regardless of the deadline of the current project. This is very helpful in time management as you get to finish assignments way before the due date so you can then accept other projects, leading to more accomplishments and earnings.

• *Learn to say "NO"*

In order to successfully manage your time as a writer, you need to learn to say a polite no to new projects. This is the most difficult lesson for the freelancers to learn as saying no to a particular project is equivalent to saying no to more income. You will proudly claim to have learned how to say no and when to say it once you look at the projects at hand and you find no project that you should not have accepted in the first place. This may be because the project is time demanding and you have limited time left in your timetable or the project is bigger than the budget attached to it. The basic point here is to learn when to say no and express it professionally, especially if you do not have time for the particular project.

• *Confidently ask questions and express yourself*

The first step in poor time management as a writer is shying away from asking questions and expressing yourself. This prevents you from asking the relevant questions regarding the deadline of the project if not indicated, clarifications for what seems unclear or if the hire is permanent or project based. These are some of the questions that are relevant in determining if you have enough time for the project or not. In addition, it is important to express yourself to the client before accepting the project. If the deadlines seem unrealistic depending on your typing speed and time available, it is possible to discuss the matter with the client and he or she can extend the deadline to suit you. This helps in proper time management that leads to achieving more in the writing career.

CHAPTER ELEVEN
Marketing Tips for Writers

Marketing is essential in making yourself known as an author, a writer, and letting others know your published books. We are going to address the marketing topic from two different dimensions namely the authors' perspective and freelancing perspective. In this way whether a freelance writer or an author, you can choose the tips that responds to your needs in your writing career.

How to Market Published Work

As an author, the writing process does not simply end with the completion of the book rather with the book finding a good market. Therefore, marking strategies are required in order to make potential customers aware of the existence of the book in the market. This entails providing catchy highlights of the contents of the book and giving them reasons as to why they need to have a copy of your book and read it. Let us now look at different viable strategies that you can use to market your published book.

- *Don't write a book...write the BEST book!*

Writing the best book is the best marketing strategy. Once you have written the best book, you can rest assured that over 90% of the marketing is already done. Best book is worth reading and sometimes it finds a favorable market even without launching vigorous campaigns for it. Writing the best books entails tapping into your talent, use of good words and developing the story progressively. In addition, inclusion of helpful content that provides direction and much needed help in making the lives of many better is a catch in writing a good book that is likely to be accepted easily in the market. The idea behind writing a best selling book is that it builds your name as an author so that the next book you write will be already advertised by the previous one. In this case, ensure that every book you write is better than the previous one in order to maintain your name as an author in the best seller books category. However, it is advisable to write your first three books before embarking on the marketing campaigns for them.

- *Identify the target readers correctly*

In order to effectively market your published book, it is important to correctly identify your target readers. This helps in writing contents that are relevant to them hence giving them a good reason to read your particular book. In this case, it is essential to remember that not everyone will want to read your book as there is no single book that appeals to all. With this awareness, you can narrow your marketing campaigns to a specific group of people hence saving your time, energy and resources that would have been wasted through a general marketing campaign. You can reach your target reader by following the steps below;

Define your target reader as a group

You can successfully narrow down to the specific group of your target readers by identifying their demographic profile. This can be done by grouping them in terms of gender, age bracket, religious and social background among others. Once you have identified their group, identify their values and who their heroes are. When you get all this information right about your target readers, it becomes super easy to make your book appealing to them.

Identify their hang out areas

In order to effectively market the book to your target readers only, it is important to identify their popular hangout areas. This entails finding out their favorite entertainment sites, blogs containing information that appeals to them, the sites they frequent in the internet and their favorite social media platforms. This helps you in coming up with a productive strategy of communicating to them about your book as you will be aware of where to get them.

Use an appealing language

Accurate identification and profiling of your target readers is essential in making use of the right language to address them. In this case, make use of the language that they can understand and relate with. Note that the language you use to sell your book to young people is different from the one you are likely to use to pass the same message to the aging group of people. Therefore, choose the language correctly.

Create a compelling marketing copy

Creating a compelling marketing copy of your book is aimed at displaying your work and letting people know what it is all about. Remember that this requires a balance between revealing enough about the book and revealing too much. Once you reveal too much, the target readers will have no need to buy the book as they have had enough of it. Therefore, build curiosity by not what you reveal about the contents of the book rather by that what you hinted about without revealing it. This is what will make the target readers buy the book as soon as possible.

Make the book readily available

Making your book readily available to readers is a key marketing strategy. Remember that through your marketing campaigns one may have the urge to read your book but forget it as soon as they realize that they cannot access it easily. Therefore, make your book available in the common online selling centers such as Amazon and eBay and other places.

How to Market Yourself as a Freelancer

As a freelancer, it is important to market yourself as you might not have own published work out there. Remember that you must start square one when others have to test your writing skills, professionalism and efficiency. Here are some tips to make you known by clients and organizations out there as a prolific writer.

Work on your profile

In the freelancing industry, the starting point is to work on your profile. This is a gradual process as you cannot build a good profile within 24hours, it may take a couple of months or a year. When building your profile ensure that your skills, experience and passion are visible to everyone who sees it. Once this is done, it is time now to successfully complete projects that will provide good ratings and attractive reviews. It is important to note that a compelling profile is made up of client reviews and portfolios attached to it. The more good reviews you have affirming your ability to provide quality work, professionalism and efficiency the better your profile becomes.

In an interview on successful profile building, Peter had the following to say;

> *"When I started writing on oDesk platform, I did not have any single review as I was just a beginner. I thought that putting a cute photo of myself and beautifully describing my skills would earn me a well paying project. Well, this was half true but I realized that I needed to take more time in working on my profile instead of focusing on making more money. I started working on projects that would earn me $1 per 500 words. This was pretty low pay but all I wanted is to gain experience and reviews for my profile. I went up gradually as my profile improved in terms of experience and referrals from clients till now I have over 100 reviews on my freelancing profile. Today, I do not work for subcontracts as clients have faith in my ability to handle their assignments effectively thanks to my good profile."*

Therefore, focus your energy and skills in building your profile that markets you to other clients.

Target working for clients not writers

In freelancing, there are two categories of people who are likely to hire your writing services. There are clients who own projects and writers who are contracted to handle the projects but prefers creating subcontracts with other writers. When writing for the clients it is rewarding as they build trust in your writing ability so that whenever they get new projects, they will always call on you. In addition, it is rewarding because the clients provide reasonable deadlines that help you to handle the existing assignments effectively. Also, you can be assured that a client will pay the full amount for the particular project.

On the other hand, if you work for fellow writers, the clients will not get to know you as all the credit will go to the writer who has hired you. At the same time the deadlines will be shorter than the one set by the client as they will have to review your work before wiring it to their client. This makes you work under pressure causing frustration. Then, the monetary gains are not rewarding as you are likely to get peanuts for the project done.

Therefore, work for clients in order to market yourself effectively, rather than for your fellow writers as you will not get known by project owners.

Post blogs

Blog posting is a prime way of marketing yourself as a freelancer to potential clients. In this case, you can work towards owning a blog on which you can make many posts of your written work. In addition write blogs and post in other blog sites letting readers know who you are. This creates opportunities for you to get hired by clients to write posts for them.

Open social media accounts

Social media platforms are one of the effective marketing tools for the freelancers. Don't use social media just for leisure chatting but to market your writing skills out there. Be creative enough to initiate dialogue that is likely to go viral hence gaining a multitude of followers and later using the platform to market products for companies. In this case, you need to be proactive in sending proposals to companies letting them know that you have a social media account with many followers and your ability to write descriptions for their products and uploading them in the social media platform. This markets your writing career.

Contact your former clients regularly

The mistake that many freelancers do is going silent after a project is completed. This can create an impression to the client that you are no longer interested in working on a similar project. Instead, contact your former clients after a short while letting them know that you are available for more projects. This prompts them to make referrals that promote your writing career greatly.

Be available long term

Once a client hires you for the first time, in most cases it is usually on short term basis. You have the power to let the client know that you are available for long term engagement. Here, you need to be creative in finding words with which to communicate with your clients at the end of the project to express your joy of having worked with them. This gives you an opportunity to express your desire to work with them on regular basis. This opens up regular job opportunities for you.

Market yourself when busy

A common mistake in marketing that freelancers make is going underground when they have a lot of work. Do not be blinded by the current workload and get into a comfort zone instead of marketing yourself. For example, you might be busy a particular week with numerous projects to complete. Despite the huge workload, think of the following week and call for other assignments to keep you busy as well in that week. Therefore, market yourself continuously for consistent income.

CHAPTER TWELVE
Facts about Publishing a Book

Book publishing entails proofreading, editing, page design, printing for the books to be sold as hand copies or uploading for the eBooks, marketing and publicity of the book. This is a complex task that requires a certain level of skills in order to publish a book that is shelf worthy. There has been a big debate on whether it is good for the authors to consider self-publishing or traditional publishing.

Self-publishing as the name goes entails taking up the role played by the editor and you as the author preparing the book. This has been made possible by the availability of software that makes the process less tedious. On the other hand, traditional publishing entails involving an editorial company in the process.

• **Advantages of Traditional Publishing**

• *Cost effective*

Traditional publishing is cost effective compared to self-publishing depending on the circumstances. In traditional publishing, the complete script of the book is entrusted to an editor who proofreads and edits the book making it ready for cover designing and printing or uploading. If you choose self publishing, it is important to remember that you might be required to repeat the same process several times or even print the entire book, only to realize some existing major mistakes in it. This becomes very expensive in long term. Therefore, it is advisable to go for traditional publishing as an editor has the experience in identifying errors and completing the job within a short period of time hence being cost effective. This makes it possible to have your complete book launched in the market at the intended time.

• *Advance allocation*

When you entrust your complete book to a publisher, you can rest assured of getting some advances. The amount provided depends on whether you are an author of bestselling books who gets a large allocation of advance or not. Nonetheless, as a first time author, the trade publisher will always allocate an advance that helps you in starting the process of writing the next book as you await for your book to start selling. This is a privilege that you will miss should you choose self publishing as you have to wait until your book sells in the market to start getting income. This might block you from moving on with the next book.

• *Editor's advice*

An editor's advice is vital when publishing the book for income generation. Editors are experienced so they can tell whether there are some aspects of the book that you need to change in order to make it sell in the market. By choosing traditional publishing, you open up the opportunities of tapping the experience and expertise of the editors. This is essential for the current book being published as well as the others to follow as it adds to your knowledge and skills. However, choosing to self publish limits your expertise to only what you know. This might make the market narrow for your book as you do not have the experience of the market and what exactly it takes for a book to sell out there. This is why it is advisable to go the traditional way of publishing compared to self publishing especially for the first time authors.

- *Credibility and legitimacy*

It is important to know that your book is likely to gain credibility and legitimacy among readers if it is approved by a publisher with a brand name in the market. In this case as a beginner in book writing, it is advisable to venture into traditional publishing in order to gain credibility and legitimacy in the market. This does not only favor your first book but also the others that will follow. On the other hand if you choose the self publishing method, you will need resources, time and energy to gain legitimacy and credibility in the market.

- *Quality control by experts*

Choosing traditional publishing methods allows the experts to control the quality of your book. This makes your book have an edge in the market as they ensure that the launched book meets the desired quality. Here, the experts control each step in the process of the publication of the book. They ensure that the best editors scrutinize your entire book. They also ensure that the typesetting, layout and cover design is handled by professional designers with experience while the publisher covers all the cost. In addition, once the book is printed or uploaded, the expert marketers are assigned to create publicity of the book accessing the market. This ensures that the published book is of high quality and delivered into the market through the best channel. This is not possible with the self publishing option.

- **Caution**

Though there are numerous advantages in using the traditional publishing method, it is important to note that the process can be slow at time. Should your chosen publisher delay the process, you have a right to withdraw and identify a new one. However, note that the publisher have up to 18 months to publish your book. In addition, in case you hand over your book to a publisher who seems to be proposing changes in the book that drifts from the original message you intended for your target readers, it is always prudent to move to a different publisher who will be ready to work with the original theme of your book. Ways of Creating an Audio Book

Audio books are not common in the market as most of the writers concentrate on books that can be read either as hand copies or eBooks. However, audio books can be an additional source of income for an author. This kind of book can be ideal for those with visual impairment as well as those who are not fond of reading. Audio books are also read widely by those too busy to sit and read a book as they can listen to an audio book while driving, doing other house chores or during a lunch break at their work place. You can notice that with the increasing demand on production when time is never enough for many, audio books are becoming more popular. In fact, you can generate an audio book from the existing written copy. Wondering how to go about it? Just read on for some tips.

What are the important factors to consider when coming up with an audio book?

In order to successfully come up with an audio book, the following factors are to be considered.

- *Does a written book exist?*

This is a key question that you need to ask yourself when planning to come up with an audio book. This is because if you have an existing written book the process becomes shorter as you do not have to write down the entire book before making it into an audio book. In case you do not have an existing book it is important to decide whether you want to have a fiction or non-fiction audio book. In addition, you need to decide whether you want to have both written and audio books. It is advisable to have both for wide source of income by having the hard copies, eBooks and audio books that are the same. Here, you need to be ready to go through the normal writing process before converting it into an audio book.

- *How to read the contents*

In order to generate an audio book, it is vital to consider how to read the contents. This is because the written contents will need to be read to create the audio format. This is the most essential part in preparing an audio book. In this case, it is important to practice how to read and pronounce words without any accent that can block the one listening to the book from hearing clearly the words. This entails learning the art of the spoken word. If the book is non-fiction, it is important to read it yourself as the author, as it creates a sense of authenticity. On the other hand, for the fiction book, you need to identify an actor or actress who has the art of pronouncing the words in figurative language and evoking the necessary emotions from the listener. The way you read the book determines the destiny of the audio book that you generate, as the punctuations, pronunciations and tone variations need to be regarded during the reading process.

- *Scripting*

Scripting is the process of reworking the book in order to add natural pauses while emphasizing certain words. Scripting should be done before the reading process in order to mark the script to be read for the reader to know when to pause or add tone variation. In addition, it helps in breaking the long sentences present in the book. This makes the reading process fluent, as required for an audio book.

- *Availability of audio publisher*

Remember that for the eBook and hard copy a book publisher is required. However, an audio publisher will be required for this type of book. The publisher guides the recording process ensuring that the recorded work meets the required standards. Therefore, identify the audio publisher to work with before, during and after the recording process.

CHAPTER THIRTEEN
Steps in creating an audio book

Once the above considerations have been made, it is the time now to create the audio book. Here are some helpful steps to follow;

Identify a sound recording location

> The first and most important step in the process of creating an audio book is identifying the sound recording location. This entails finding the best room in which you are to conduct the recording without the interference by external noise, room echoes and ambient noises that leads to poor recording. This requires enough research before the due date of recordings in order to identify the ideal location for a clear noise free recording. If you cannot locate a recording studio, then you can improvise one right in your house. A good suggestion is a closet full of clothes, as the clothes will absorb the background noise for a clear recording.

Gather the recording tools

> It is important to ensure that you have the right recording tools that are functional. In this case, you need to have an iPad and an external microphone. You can consider having an apogee Mic which is advisable as it is compatible with the iPad and external microphone hence producing the desired sound for an excellent audio book. In addition, making use of the Garage Band for ios helps in getting a clear voice recording.

Offload the recorded files to iTunes

> The importance of using the Garage band is that it facilitates offloading of the recorded audio files to iTunes. In this case, you should offload the files to iTunes when you complete a reading of each chapter. This is an easy to do job when using an iPad as all you need to do is to tap on the recorded files in the iPad and then select to share files with iTunes Library located on the Mac. This helps in ensuring that the recordings made are safe as you proceed with other chapters as it may take a while before completely reading the entire book.

Editing the recorded files

> Garage Band on the Mac makes it possible for you to edit the recorded audio files. This helps in eliminating the parts of the audio that are not required. This possibility gives you the freedom to read a sentence twice or allow some interruption as you can cut them out through editing. The possibility of editing the recorded work enables you to read the entire book while relaxed without the fear of making mistakes as you can correct them without interfering with all the files.

Wrap up the chapters into a single audio book

Once you are satisfied that the editing is complete, it is advisable to give the files to a second person to listen to it. The role of the second listener is to ascertain that the recorded files have a flow hence confirming that the listeners to your book will not have issues with its flow. When the affirmation is granted by a second listener, you can go ahead and wrap up the entire book into a single whole. In the Mac App store, there is an audio book binder that effectively combines all the chapters of the recorded audio files into a complete audio book.

CHAPTER FOURTEEN
How to Create Multiple Streams of Income through Writing

Writing is not a hobby but a career with full potential of expanding just like any other business. You can create multiple streams of income through writing and become financially stable. However, one more thing is necessary….get out of your comfort zone! This happens only when you decide to work hard but smart. If you take writing as a hobby, you will not have the urge to break through the visible boundaries and venture into unknown in the writing industry. Therefore, let it be your career and business that you need to think out of the box and do new things for the expansion of the business. Here are different suggestions on how to open up multiple streams of income through writing.

- *Freelancing*

Freelancing seems an obvious way of making income through writing. Freelancing is a good starting point in writing though you need to up the game in order to make meaningful income. Let us be realistic, you cannot adequately pay your bills by writing content for $1-$10 per 500. Well, it is good for the start but you need to make a conscious decision to break away from this low pay. It is not a walk in the park but it takes time, patience and determination to venture into other places. Most freelancers depend on job mill centers and major freelancing platforms to bid for the jobs.

However, this is not the only way as you can create your own blog and post materials on it, advertising your skills to potential clients who pay well. In addition, you can post blogs as a guest blogger on some sites that makes people know what you can offer in their companies. You get the payment worth the hours and type of the project you have handled for the client. In the job mills, the clients will go for the lowest bidder making it difficult to find a well paying client. In addition, helping the clients to discover you through guest posting of the materials, you are likely to get referred to other potential clients.

- *Book writing*

As a writer, you can combine content writing with book writing. You can dedicate five hours each day to handle the blog assignments while the rest of the time you concentrate in book writing. This results in two sources of income as the books continue to sell in the market and your blog writing career brings in additional income. However, this requires dedication and hard work as well as good time management. This may open up yet a third source of income as motivational speakers and experts in different fields can hire you to put the information they already have from their conferences into a book format. This is an easy job to do that does not necessarily interfere with the normal assignment of writing blogs.

- *Work for companies around you*

When you become a freelancer, it's easy to forget about the job opportunities within your locality. This is ideal for people living in areas with manufacturing companies and other service providing companies. As a freelancer, you do not have to be employed as a full time writer, but more on a contract based per project. In order to achieve this, you need to tarmac so that you can present your proposal. I understand that time is a limited factor for freelancers so you can collect email addresses and write to the companies introducing yourself as a freelance writer. Highlight your skills in product description, marketing campaign preparation and launching as well as blog writing for the SEO of their business website. In this case, it is important to write a sample description of one of their products for their review and allow them to make use of it free of charge. This makes them aware of the skills that you are likely to contribute in their company. The executive may realize the need of hiring you other than having a full time marketer for their company. This creates an opportunity for you to make additional income for a company located just down the street from your home.

- *Transcription*

Many writers shy away from transcription services as they seem complicated. However, this can become an additional source of income for a writer. Transcription entails listening and watching recorded audio and video files respectively while transferring information into text format. This job can be a walk in the park, especially for an experienced writer with good headphones to listen and capture the words in the files accurately. You can get more clients especially in the education field for the transcription of research interviews and lectures, from the health field, legal, broadcasting companies and businesses. This is becoming an increasingly important service due to advancement of online businesses that are making use of podcasts as marketing tools.

CHAPTER FIFTHTEEN
How to Become a Better Writer

Becoming a better writer should be the endeavor of every individual involved in a writing career. This is because without better skills it is difficult to build your career and create other streams of income with the aim of becoming financially stable. Apart from continuous practice in writing, you need to be 100% committed in improving your skills in order to be a professional. Writing is a craft that has to be nurtured, with creativity being a crown to it. Possessing great writing skills make it possible for potential clients to locate you and build trust in your ability to deliver quality projects. Here are tips in making your writing skills better.

- *Read widely*

The first step in becoming a better writer each single day is through reading widely. As a writer, you need to expand your reading beyond newspapers, journals and newsletters to blogs written by other bloggers and books. This helps in tapping into the writing styles of other people especially those who have excelled in the industry. In addition, it helps in improving your grammar especially if you are not from a native English speaking background. Reading materials written by natives helps in gaining the structure and tone of a native speaker, convincing clients and readers of your work that you can write content just like that from native English speaking regions. This gives you a competitive edge as a potential client just has to look at your writing style, grammar and tone used in the content to gain confidence that you are the right person for the job.

> ○ *When I am handling assignments as well as during my leisure time, I have found it helpful to read what other writers have posted online. In this case, I concentrate on a particular topic, exploring how several bloggers have approached the same topic. In this case, I relay on sites like www.ezinearticles.com, www.amazon.com or www.ebay.com for information. In addition, I ensure that I browse into other business blogs on various topics hence getting ideas on how to formulate tittles for the articles, the structures and facts about the topic in questions. This has helped me in handling assignments as sometimes clients entrust projects on niches that I am not familiar with. In this case, I do not reject the assignments but I commit myself to read widely on the topics hence succeeding in completing the assignments.*

- *Rewriting Newspaper or magazine articles*

If you are a writing beginner, you can improve your skills by rewriting articles in the newspapers and magazines. This can be an exercise that helps you to generate samples to attach in the job application during the bidding process. Rewriting articles sharpens your scanning skills through a portion of materials provided and identifying the key points. These are the points that you use to come up with a unique article that passes the plagiarism test. In addition, this helps in increasing your typing speed as you start taking less time to scan through the researched materials for a given project thus completing the assignments before the set deadlines. Rewriting of existing articles helps you to discover your writing style that you develop as time goes by.

- *Join a writers' club*

If you are serious about improving your writing skills, it is important to join a writers' club. There are numerous writers' clubs available online that accept membership. This becomes a platform in which you can share your writing and receive honest feedback from other experienced writers. While they offer suggestions on areas that you need to work on in order to improve your writing. The club also mentors you on how to up your game in the writing career as well as ways of getting good clients for career advancement. It is important to note that some of the writers' clubs do charge a membership fee that varies from one group to the other, while others are free of charge. A good example of a writers' club is About Writing Squared-The 5 Buck Forum. This is a paid forum for freelancers who form a community that is active and very supportive to its members. However, it is advisable to search for more forums in order to settle on the one that works best for you. In these forums, you get mentored into a writer of best-seller content.

- *Comment on blogs*

It is important to embark on commenting on blogs posted by other bloggers on different sites. This gives you the skills of evaluating blogs thus being able to identify the best blog among numerous good ones. This is a simple exercise that does not take much of your time as you just need to comment "mmm…good piece of work" "Nice post there!" This gives you the ability to check on your own blogs and identify areas of improvement in order to become a good writer. It is through evaluating other people's blogs that you learn what it takes to be a good writer. So do not just comment but learn!

- *Take part in writing prompts*

Writing prompts refers to creative writing challenges and writing exercises offered by different providers. These challenges vary from short articles to full novel writing tests such us writing a novel in 30 days. These writing prompts are available online and they help you in improving your general writing as well as story development and arrangement of ideas to create a good flow in a piece of writing. However, it is advisable not to take the challenge with the aim of winning as you may get discouraged but have the main aim as improving your writing skills.

- *Increase you targets each day*

Daily targets of the words written helps in improving writing skills. This is essential for the beginners as it prepares them to handle volumes of workload daily. You can start with a target of 500 words daily before starting to take in assignments and increasing it to 1,000 words. Then as you gain experience, target at writing 2,000 words daily. When you achieve this, then it is time to start accepting multiple assignments as you can write about 5 articles of 500 words each day. However, you should not stop at this as you can continue setting targets for yourself until you can type about 6,000 words daily.

CHAPTER SIXTEEN
A Must to Have Resources for a Successful Writing Career

As we come near to the conclusion of this book, it is important to explore the must have resources for a successful writing career. As we said before writing is a business, though a different type of business. This is because it is not capital extensive, so you can start with a minimal investment according to your financial ability. Here are the resources required to start:

- *A computer*

The most important resource to start a writing career is a functioning computer. You can consider having either a desktop or a laptop computer for the job. If you choose to have a desktop computer, ensure that it has a good keyboard to facilitate typing. The computer should have normal programs to start with. Other software can be added as you progress in your writing career such as plagiarism testers and readability software among others. However, if you travel a lot for different reasons, it is important to get a laptop so you can work from any location.

- *Internet connection*

Adequate internet connection is a major resource in starting a writing career. The internet connection helps you to connect with the clients effectively in discussing the details of the assignments, researching for the assignment and wiring the complete assignments. Therefore, you need to identify a reliable internet provider for efficiency in a writing career.

- *Research skills*

Research skills are essential in starting a writing career. This entails a good knowledge of the prime sites for information and blogs that are essential for getting enough facts for successful completion of the projects. It is essential to have the ability to navigate through a browser to areas that are likely to have the materials needed. Sites such as www.amazon.com, www.ebay.com and www.ezinearticles.com among others can really help you in improving your research skills.

- *Headphones*

It is important to have a pair of headphones that are functioning adequately. Headphones come in handy in case of live interviews over Skype. They are also essential for the audio files provided as references for a given assignment. In addition, they are vital for transcription services of recorded audio and video files as you will need to listen and type each spoken word in the provided files. This will make your work very efficient.

- *Social media accounts*

As a writer, it is important to have several social media accounts for effective communication and other uses. In this case, it is advisable to have a Gmail account that offers a possibility to communicate through Gtalk. In addition, you need to have a Twitter, Facebook and LinkedIn account for necessary job links that can become part of a strategy for extra income when you get numerous followings as you can market products for clients. Skype is a must have for a writing career for effective communication with clients and mentors.

Conclusion

Writing should not be treated as a hobby but as a business and a career. Though it comes with a host of challenges in the beginning, it is rewarding in terms of the returns and the freedom in time management. Earning a living from writing is an option for many globally, at this time when the job market in the formal employment sector is flooded. Do not fear letting the world know that you have a talent in writing with a creative mind, as this can be the beginning of a bright writing career. The different tips on how to become a good writer, how to type fast and the top mistakes to avoid among other helpful hints will surely help you climb to great heights. With your determination and resilience, you can become the writer you dream of. Do not shy away….go for it; it's yours for taking!

www.ingramcontent.com/pod-product-compliance
Lightning Source LLC
Chambersburg PA
CBHW080610180526
45168CB00007B/2860